THE UNOFFI[CIAL]
BIBL[E]
FOR
MINECRAFTERS
LIFE OF MOSES

GARRETT ROMINES AND CHRISTOPHER MIKO

STORIES FROM THE BIBLE
TOLD BLOCK BY BLOCK

LION

Text copyright © 2016 Christopher Miko and Garrett Romines
Illustrations copyright © 2016 Christopher Miko and Garrett Romines
This mini edition copyright © 2018 Lion Hudson IP Limited

The right of Christopher Miko and Garrett Romines to be identified as the authors and illustrators of this work has been asserted by them in accordance with the Copyright, Designs and Patents Act 1988.

Published by
Lion Hudson Limited
Wilkinson House, Jordan Hill Business Park,
Banbury Road, Oxford OX2 8DR, England
www.lionhudson.com

ISBN 978 0 7459 7742 3

Original Bible edition published by Sky Pony Press, 307 West 36th Street, 11th Floor, New York, NY 10018

Stories originally published in *The Unofficial Old Testament for Minecrafters* and *The Unofficial New Testament for Minecrafters* 2016
This mini edition 2018

Acknowledgments
A catalogue record for this book is available from the British Library
Minecraft ® is a registered trademark of Notch Development AB.
The Minecraft ® game is copyright © Mojang AB.

Printed and bound in China, June 2018, LH54

CONTENTS

FOREWORD   IV

MOSES GROWS UP   1

MOSES AND THE PLAGUES   11

THE PARTING OF THE RED SEA   26

THE TEN COMMANDMENTS   31

THE BATTLE OF JERICHO   37

FOREWORD

I'm always on the lookout for new ways to tell Bible stories. That's what storytellers do. The hardest job is finding a compelling and original "way in" to a story. And when I find something that works, I get really excited.

My grandchildren are mad keen on Minecraft ®. They don't get much game-playing time, but when they do, Minecraft ® is their first choice. The older two (nine and six) love building the worlds, while the youngest, who is only three, simply enjoys digging holes and getting stuck in them.

So when I showed them a few sample pages from *The Unofficial Bible for Minecrafters* their responses ranged from "It's funny" (which it is!) to "When can I read some more?"

As for me, I turned the pages just to see what the creators of the book would get up to next and how they would bring each scene to Minecrafter-life. And I have to say that I was surprised and delighted.

Every now and then, someone comes up with a new way of telling Bible stories that is just that little bit different. And if this is a "way in" for someone (and there are thousands of Minecrafters out there) and it's compelling, intriguing, and faithful to the text, then I'm happy to recommend it. That's what storytellers do.

Bob Hartman

Bob Hartman, Storyteller

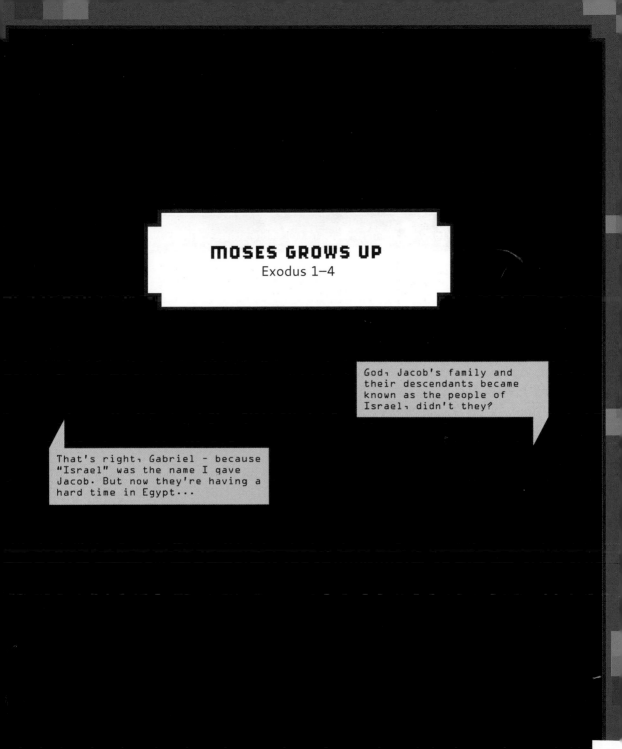

MOSES GROWS UP
Exodus 1–4

God, Jacob's family and their descendants became known as the people of Israel, didn't they?

That's right, Gabriel - because "Israel" was the name I gave Jacob. But now they're having a hard time in Egypt...

THE NUMBER OF ISRAELITES IN EGYPT WAS GREATLY INCREASING AND THEY BECAME VERY POWERFUL.

A NEW PHARAOH CAME TO THE THRONE OF EGYPT. HE FELT OVERWHELMED BY THE NUMBER OF ISRAELITES IN HIS COUNTRY.

The Israelites have become too many and too strong. We must make sure they don't wage war against us.

You need to take care of those boys. Do you understand my orders?

Yes, Your Majesty. I shall do as you command.

PHARAOH WAS DETERMINED TO REDUCE THE NUMBER OF ISRAELITES IN HIS LAND SO HE ANNOUNCED A DECREE THAT ALL NEWBORN ISRAELITE BOYS BE THROWN INTO THE RIVER NILE.

ONE DAY, A YOUNG ISRAELITE COUPLE HAD A BABY BOY. HIS MOTHER WAS AFRAID OF WHAT WOULD HAPPEN TO HER SON, SO SHE DECIDED TO PLACE HIM IN A BASKET THAT WOULD FLOAT DOWN THE RIVER NILE.

AT THAT TIME PHARAOH'S DAUGHTER CAME TO BATHE IN THE RIVER NILE. SHE RESCUED THE BABY FROM THE BASKET AND DECIDED TO RAISE THE CHILD AS HER OWN.

I will name him Moses!

GOD PROTECTED THE CHILD AS THE BASKET WENT DOWN THE RIVER. IT WAS THEN GRADUALLY CARRIED TOWARD THE RIVERBANK.

AND SO MOSES WAS BROUGHT UP BY AN EGYPTIAN PRINCESS, AND LIVED WITH PHARAOH'S FAMILY IN THE PALACE. PHARAOH TREATED HIM LIKE ONE OF HIS OWN FAMILY. WHEN MOSES HAD GROWN INTO A YOUNG MAN, HE WITNESSED AN EGYPTIAN OVERSEER STRIKING AN ISRAELITE SLAVE.

Who are you to talk, Moses? What are you going to do - kill me like you killed that Egyptian?

Stop fighting!

MOSES RUSHED IN TO STOP THE OVERSEER, AND, IN HIS ANGER, KILLED HIM. THE NEXT DAY, MOSES TRIED TO STOP TWO MEN FIGHTING, BUT REALIZED ONE OF THEM HAD WITNESSED HIS CRIME.

NOW LEAVING EGYPT. THANKS FOR COMING!

ROAD TO MIDIAN

I'm out of here!

COME AGAIN SOON

MOSES WAS AFRAID PHARAOH WOULD PUNISH HIM, SO HE RAN AWAY TO THE LAND OF MIDIAN TO START A NEW LIFE.

YEARS PASSED AND THE ISRAELITES REMAINED SLAVES. THEY CRIED OUT TO GOD FOR HELP.

MOSES WAS LIVING HAPPILY IN MIDIAN, TENDING TO HIS FLOCKS.

A bush on fire, yet it does not burn up...

ONE DAY MOSES SAW SOMETHING IN THE DISTANCE. HE LEFT HIS FLOCKS AND CLIMBED THE MOUNTAIN TO INVESTIGATE THE STRANGE LIGHT. GOD APPEARED TO HIM IN THE FLAME OF A BURNING BUSH.

MOSES MOVED CLOSER TO THE BUSH.

Moses, Moses!

Here I am.

Do not come any closer! And take off your sandals, for you are standing on holy ground.

GOD SPOKE AGAIN TO MOSES.

I am the God of your father, of Abraham, of Isaac, and of Jacob.

MOSES SHOOK AT THE WORDS OF GOD AND BOWED LOW.

I have seen the misery of my people in Egypt and I have heard their cries. I will send you to Pharaoh and you shall bring my people out of Egypt.

But who am I, that I should go to Pharaoh and bring the Israelites out of Egypt? I am just a simple man.

I will be with you. This shall be the sign that I sent you: when you have brought the people out of Egypt, you shall all worship God here on this mountain.

If I am to go to the Israelites and tell them that the God of their forefathers has sent me, and they ask me his name, what shall I say?

I AM WHO I AM. Tell them you have been sent by I AM WHO I AM!

WELCOME TO
FABULOUS EGYPT

HOME O
THE
PYRAMID

PLEASE WA
LIKE AN
EGYPTIAN

MOSES DECIDED HE WOULD DO ALL THAT GOD ASKED OF
HIM. HE LEFT HIS HOME IN MIDIAN TO RETURN TO EGYPT.

MOSES AND THE PLAGUES
Exodus 5–12

I have a feeling this doesn't bode well for the Egyptians.

Who is this that comes before Pharaoh?

It is I, Moses. I have a message for you from the God of the Israelites. He says this: "Let my people go!"

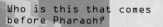

THE DAY CAME WHEN MOSES WENT BEFORE PHARAOH. HE STOOD TALL AND BRAVE.

I am Pharaoh of Egypt, a living god on Earth, and I will bow to no one!

Teach these Israelites a lesson — work them harder! I will show them who their master is.

Yes, Your Majesty.

PHARAOH WAS DETERMINED TO SHOW MOSES WHO WAS IN CHARGE. THINGS GOT MUCH WORSE FOR THE ISRAELITES.

When they make bricks, do not provide them with straw. But see to it that they make the same number of bricks as before.

How are we to make the same number of bricks without straw to fatten and strengthen them?

THE ISRAELITES PLEADED WITH PHARAOH.

With whips, you will! You can gather the straw yourselves, you lazy lot.

Lord, why have you brought pain and suffering to your people?

This is all your fault.

My life is worse now.

THE ISRAELITES BLAMED MOSES FOR THEIR TROUBLES. HE PRAYED FOR GUIDANCE.

Have no fear, Moses. I have not forgotten my promise to the people of Israel. Now watch what I do to Pharaoh!

GOD REASSURED MOSES THAT HE WOULD FREE THE ISRAELITES FROM SLAVERY.

15

God says, "Let my people go!" If Your Majesty refuses, God will send signs throughout the land of Egypt to show that he is God. And he will bring out the Israelites to freedom.

What power has been given to do this?

MOSES RETURNED TO PHARAOH.

If you wish for a sign, look at this.

MOSES THREW HIS STAFF TO THE GROUND.

Your cheap tricks will not move Pharaoh. I am supreme ruler of these lands and I will not give in to your demands or those of your God.

THE STAFF TURNED INTO A SNAKE.

THE NEXT DAY, MOSES SPOKE TO PHARAOH ON THE BANKS OF THE RIVER NILE.

MOSES TOUCHED THE WATER WITH HIS STAFF AND THE WATER TURNED TO BLOOD.

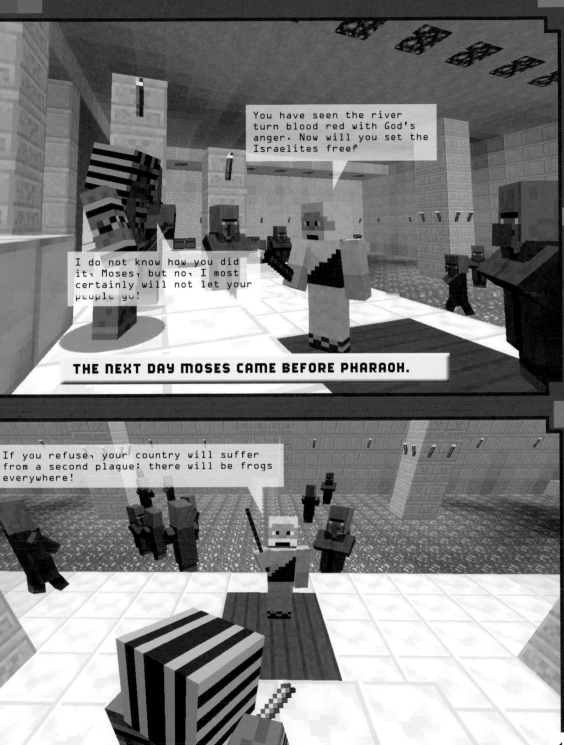

PHARAOH LOOKED OUTSIDE AND SAW THAT ALL OF EGYPT WAS COVERED IN FROGS.

This cannot be happening. Curse this God of Moses! Doesn't he know who he is dealing with? I will never bend to his will!

NEXT, GOD SENT A PLAGUE OF GNATS ONTO THE LAND, AND AGAIN PHARAOH REFUSED TO LET THE ISRAELITES GO. SO THEN GOD SENT SWARMS OF FLIES.

PHARAOH STILL DID NOT GIVE IN, SO GOD SENT PLAGUES OF DISEASE TO KILL THE ANIMALS, BOILS, AND HAIL. FINALLY, A PLAGUE OF LOCUSTS ATE ALL THAT WAS GREEN ON THE LAND, AND PLUNGED EGYPT INTO FAMINE.

GOD THEN COVERED THE LAND IN DARKNESS FOR THREE DAYS TO WARN PHARAOH THAT HE MUST RELEASE THE ISRAELITES. BUT PHARAOH STILL WOULD NOT LET THEM GO.

Your Majesty, God is ready to send the final plague, which will make you and your people greatly suffer. For God has said this: "All the firstborn of both people and animals shall die." Pharaoh - please - let my people go!

MOSES RETURNED TO SPEAK TO PHARAOH ONCE AGAIN.

I will never let my slaves go!

HATE AND ANGER SWELLED IN PHARAOH. HE UTTERED THE FATEFUL WORDS THAT DOOMED EGYPT.

SO CAME THE TENTH AND FINAL PLAGUE. GOD TOLD THE ISRAELITES TO PLACE LAMB'S BLOOD ON THEIR DOORPOSTS THAT NIGHT. THIS WOULD SHOW THE ANGEL OF DEATH WHICH HOUSEHOLDS TO SPARE.

AS THE ANGEL OF DEATH PASSED OVER EACH HOUSE THAT WAS MARKED WITH LAMB'S BLOOD, THIS BECAME KNOWN AS THE PASSOVER.

AND SO IT WAS THAT THE ANGEL OF DEATH PASSED BY THE DOORS OF THE ISRAELITES, BUT STRUCK DOWN THE FIRSTBORN CHILDREN OF ALL THE OTHER FAMILIES IN EGYPT, INCLUDING THAT OF PHARAOH.

THAT NIGHT PHARAOH SUMMONED MOSES. IT WAS CLEAR THAT PHARAOH HAD HAD A CHANGE OF HEART.

Get out, and take your people with you!

FINALLY FREE, THE ISRAELITES HASTILY SET OUT WITH MOSES TO THE LAND THAT GOD HAD PROMISED THEM.

THE PARTING OF THE RED SEA
Exodus 14

At last - freedom for the Israelites!

But they're not out of danger yet.

ONCE THE ISRAELITES HAD LEFT, PHARAOH SUDDENLY REGRETTED LOSING ALL THE SLAVES THAT HAD WORKED SO HARD FOR HIM. SO HE SUMMONED HIS SOLDIERS, AND ORDERED THEM TO PURSUE THE ISRAELITES.

Hurry! We must get our slaves back!

There they are!
Let's get them!

PHARAOH AND HIS ARMY RACED ACROSS THE DESERT IN PURSUIT OF THE ISRAELITES, AND SOON CAUGHT SIGHT OF THEM.

Moses, what have you done?
We're trapped!

Pharaoh will not show us mercy.

THE ISRAELITES WERE AT THE EDGE OF THE RED SEA. THEY WERE NOW CORNERED.

Do not be afraid. Stand firm. The God of Israel will show his power.

MOSES STRETCHED OUT HIS HAND TOWARD THE WATER,
FEELING THE PRESENCE OF GOD WITHIN HIM.

Move quickly across
the sea. God has
saved us!

Look - it's
incredible!

God has
rescued us
just in time!

THE PEOPLE WERE ASTONISHED WHEN THEY SAW THE SEA PARTING.

Your Majesty, look! By some miracle, the sea has parted and the Israelites have escaped.

They have not escaped yet. Order your men to go after them.

THE EGYPTIAN ARMY WENT INTO THE SEA AFTER THE ISRAELITES. BUT MOSES STRETCHED OUT HIS HAND AND A STRONG WIND BLEW, MAKING THE WATERS CLOSE OVER PHARAOH'S ARMY.

THE TEN COMMANDMENTS

Exodus 19–20; Deuteronomy 5

It's time to give the Israelites instructions on how to live a good and holy life.

MOSES AND THE PEOPLE OF ISRAEL JOURNEYED ON IN SEARCH OF THEIR HOMELAND. MOSES LED THE PEOPLE TO THE FOOT OF MOUNT SINAI. THERE GOD WOULD MAKE A COVENANT WITH THEM.

Moses, come up to the top of the mountain. But make sure the people stay down below.

GOD SUMMONED MOSES TO THE TOP OF THE MOUNTAIN. AND SO HE BEGAN THE LONG CLIMB UP.

WHEN HE COULD CLIMB NO HIGHER, MOSES TOOK ONE LAST LOOK AT THE PEOPLE OF ISRAEL. THEN HE STEPPED OUT OF SIGHT AND WENT TO SPEAK WITH GOD.

HIGH UP ON THE MOUNTAIN, ALL WAS QUIET. SUDDENLY, MOSES HEARD GOD'S VOICE.

I
YOU SHALL HAVE
NO GOD BESIDES
ME

II
YOU SHALL NOT
MAKE CARVED
IMAGES OF GODS

III
YOU SHALL NOT
MISUSE GOD'S
NAME

IV
YOU SHALL
REMEMBER THE
SABBATH DAY

V
YOU SHALL HONOUR
YOUR FATHER
AND MOTHER

VI
YOU SHALL NOT
COMMIT MURDER

VII
YOU SHALL NOT
COMMIT ADULTERY

VIII
YOU SHALL NOT
STEAL

IX
YOU SHALL
NOT BEAR
FALSE WITNESS

X
YOU SHALL
NOT COVET

Moses, I am the Lord your God who brought you out of Egypt. I give you these laws to live by.

Guide me in your ways.

GOD CARVED THESE TEN COMMANDMENTS INTO TWO TABLETS OF STONE. HE ALSO GAVE MOSES INSTRUCTIONS ON HOW TO LIVE A GOOD LIFE AND HOW TO WORSHIP HIM. HE SAID THE HOLY TABLETS MUST BE KEPT IN A SPECIAL BOX, THE ARK OF THE COVENANT.

I
YOU SHALL HAVE
NO GOD BESIDES
ME

II
YOU SHALL NOT
MAKE CARVED
IMAGES OF GODS

III
YOU SHALL NOT
MISUSE GOD'S
NAME

IV
YOU SHALL
REMEMBER THE
SABBATH DAY

V
YOU SHALL
HONOUR
YOUR FATHER
AND MOTHER

VI
YOU SHALL NOT
COMMIT MURDER

VII
YOU SHALL NOT
COMMIT ADULTERY

VIII
YOU SHALL NOT
STEAL

IX
YOU SHALL
NOT BEAR
FALSE WITNESS

X
YOU SHALL
NOT COVET

Return to my people and give them these commandments.

MOSES THEN LEFT THE MOUNTAIN AND BROUGHT THE TABLETS DOWN TO THE PEOPLE.

THE BATTLE OF JERICHO

Numbers 27; Deuteronomy 31;
Joshua 1–4, 6

Good work on the commandments!

Thank you. Whether they'll keep them is another matter!

So, who led them after Moses?

I told Moses to choose his friend Joshua.

IT DID NOT TAKE LONG FOR THE PEOPLE OF ISRAEL TO BREAK GOD'S LAWS,
SO HE PREVENTED THEM FROM ENTERING THE LAND OF CANAAN. THEY HAD
TO WANDER IN THE DESERT FOR FORTY YEARS. EVEN MOSES HIMSELF WAS
DISOBEDIENT TO GOD AND WAS NOT ALLOWED TO ENTER CANAAN. AFTER
MOSES DIED, HIS GREAT FRIEND JOSHUA BECAME THE LEADER OF THE
ISRAELITES.

GOD THEN SPOKE TO JOSHUA AND
TOLD HIM THAT THE PEOPLE OF
ISRAEL COULD FINALLY CROSS
THE RIVER JORDAN AND ENTER
CANAAN. HE PROMISED THAT IF
THEY FOLLOWED HIS LAWS, HE
WOULD GUARANTEE VICTORY OVER
ALL THEIR ENEMIES.

JOSHUA BEGAN TO LEAD THE ISRAELITES INTO THE PROMISED LAND, BUT A GREAT CITY STOOD IN THEIR WAY: THE CITY OF JERICHO. IF THEY WANTED TO REACH THE LAND OF CANAAN, THEY WOULD HAVE TO CONQUER JERICHO FIRST.

Speak to the people and find out what we need to know. Then leave as quietly as possible.

JOSHUA SUMMONED TWO OF HIS BRAVEST MEN. HE ASKED THEM TO GO SECRETLY INTO JERICHO TO FIND OUT WHETHER THE CITY WAS GOOD OR BAD, AND WHETHER IT WOULD BE AN ENEMY OF ISRAEL.

I have heard that there are
spies in the city, Your Majesty.

They must not be allowed to escape.
I order their immediate capture!

**NO SOONER HAD THE TWO ISRAELITE SPIES ENTERED THE CITY, THAN
THE KING OF JERICHO ORDERED THE MEN TO BE CAPTURED.**

Will she
help us?

We will see...

Can you hide us?

Yes, but you must be as
quiet as mice. The guards
may search the house.

**THE TWO SPIES SAW THE
SOLDIERS COMING AND
RAN TO THE HOUSE OF A
WOMAN NAMED RAHAB.**

**SHE HID THE MEN IN THE STRAW
THAT COVERED HER ROOF.**

RAHAB LET THE MEN DOWN A ROPE OUTSIDE THE CITY WALLS.

We have seen the city and it can be taken. The people live in fear of us.

We nearly got caught, but a woman helped us. We promised no harm would come to her or her family.

How will we know who she is?

She will hang a red cord out of her window.

THE SPIES RETURNED TO JOSHUA AND TOLD HIM ABOUT THEIR JOURNEY.

JOSHUA'S ARMY MARCHED TOWARD JERICHO. BETWEEN THE ISRAELITES AND JERICHO WAS THE MIGHTY RIVER JORDAN. IT WAS TOO BIG AND DEEP FOR THEM TO CROSS.

JOSHUA INSTRUCTED THE PRIESTS TO CARRY THE ARK OF THE COVENANT TO THE WATER. AS SOON AS THE PRIESTS' FEET TOUCHED THE RIVER, THE WATERS DIVIDED AND THE PEOPLE CROSSED ON DRY LAND.

TWELVE STONES WERE PLACED ON THE RIVER BED AND TWELVE ON THE SHORE IN CANAAN TO REMIND THE PEOPLE OF WHAT GOD HAD DONE.

SOON AFTERWARDS JOSHUA SAW AN ANGEL OF THE LORD. THE ANGEL SAID THAT HE HAD BEEN SENT BY GOD TO TELL JOSHUA HOW TO DEFEAT THE POWERFUL CITY OF JERICHO.